Original title:
Vines Across the Ceiling

Copyright © 2025 Creative Arts Management OÜ
All rights reserved.

Author: Zachary Prescott
ISBN HARDBACK: 978-1-80581-757-4
ISBN PAPERBACK: 978-1-80581-284-5
ISBN EBOOK: 978-1-80581-757-4

Ethereal Green Blooms

In the corner, plants entwine,
Doing the tango, oh so fine.
Climbing high, they seek the light,
Making shadows dance at night.

Hanging pots with tangled dreams,
Whisper secrets, or so it seems.
They gossip low, the leaves unite,
With personalities, oh what a sight!

Each leaf sways with so much sass,
Like they're at a garden class.
Charming bees with floral cheer,
Buzzing laughs, they've got no fear.

If I could swing from ceiling high,
I'd join the greenery, oh my!
Sipping sun and laughing loud,
In this leafy, quirky crowd.

Threads of Nature's Quilt

A patchwork of green upon the beams,
Sewing stories, weaving dreams.
Each leaf a patch, a tale to tell,
In this fabric, all's quite swell.

They somersault and twist about,
Daring lights to shine, no doubt.
Like circus tricks, they play their part,
Nature's jesters, pure heart art.

Hanging down like playful quirks,
Leaping with the morning larks.
Who knew green could be so fun?
Dancing shadows, second to none.

In this fabric of life we share,
Every twig brings laughter, rare.
So here's to the ceiling's green delight,
Where nature's choirs sing through the night.

The Green Embrace

In a room with ceilings high,
A green army crawls, oh my!
Tangled limbs dance in delight,
As they peek through in twilight.

Hats on these leafy legs they wear,
Pants of ivy, beyond compare.
They hold a party, jazz in shades,
Who knew plants could serenade?

Trailing Light and Leaf

A light bulb shines, they reach to play,
With shadows that swirl night and day.
Their tendrils twist, a circus act,
Above your head, a leafy pact.

They whisper jokes to dust and time,
Comedic roots in nature's rhyme.
And if you listen, you'll hear their cheer,
As laughter grows, they shed a tear.

Whispering Growth Above

With a giggle, the green folks creep,
Over my head, they hardly sleep.
They tickle ears with playful pranks,
And hand out leaves like banked-out flanks.

One remarked, 'I'm not a weed!'
As I stumbled through their leafy creed.
'We're gardeners too with secrets untold,
Just wait till your shoes are three shades of gold!'

Interlocking Nature

Up in the rafters, a leafy crew,
Hatching plans for a rave or two.
With ivy-twirls and laughter wide,
Creating a jungle where fun can hide.

Their roots entwine like best friends tight,
In a green embrace, what a sight!
They joke of soil, forgetting the dirt,
While plotting a party, who'll wear the skirt?

Climbing Spirals of Hope

Twisted tendrils dance with glee,
Reaching for the light they see.
A sock caught high, oh what a sight,
Hanging there, a silly plight.

Green fingers stretch and bend with grace,
Tickling roofs in a cheeky chase.
Does the ceiling mind the fun?
Or is this mischief never done?

Chasing Sunlight Above

In corners where the dust bunnies lay,
A leafy leggy race starts to play.
Each leaf a hat, jaunty and bright,
Soon to topple, oh what a fright!

Climbing higher with each bold step,
Grabbing curtains, what a misrep!
They giggle as they snag a shoe,
Is it yours, or mine, or just brand new?

Flourish Amongst the Stars

Reaching for cosmos with leafy dreams,
Whispering wishes in silken beams.
A rogue pot crashes, thud with flair,
Who knew plants could cause such despair?

Undersecurity, a wild king,
Bouncing about with a leaf-clad swing.
Stars look down and curiously ask,
"If they're that high, who's to bask?"

Embracing the Overhead

Clinging tight to the faulted beams,
Curtains shudder in leafy dreams.
A playful knot, a tangled mess,
Eclectic art, who'd dare to guess?

Laughing quietly, they sway with ease,
Sharing secrets in the gentle breeze.
The ceiling frowns, but don't despair,
For these green jesters bring fun to the air!

Ascent of Nature

In the corner, plants take a stroll,
Climbing high, playing their role.
A leafy parade on the wall,
Whispering secrets, having a ball.

Green tendrils stretching for the light,
They wriggle and giggle, a comical sight.
Hanging from hooks like they own the place,
Nature's jesters, a leafy embrace.

Tiny flowers join the show,
Bright colors pop, putting on a glow.
They sway and dance, with flair so grand,
Nature's party, a leafy band.

So here we gather, both humans and leaves,
Amidst the laughter, no room for grieves.
With potting soil and joy to share,
Life's a joke, and we're all unaware.

The Lattice of Life

Twisting and twirling, they reach for the sky,
Like acrobats swinging, oh my, oh my!
A comedy act without any fear,
Dropping their leaves like confetti here.

A web of green, a playful sight,
Hanging about, ready for a fight.
They tangle and tustle in a fun little game,
Who knew nature could be so lame?

The insects join, with chuckles and chirps,
A bustling crowd, no need for any burps.
In this lattice of life, humor unfolds,
Old jokes retold, and new ones bold.

So let's raise a glass to the leafy jokes,
To clumsy plants and silly folks.
They're climbing higher, taking the stage,
In the comedy of life, they're the best on page.

Twilight's Embrace

As sunlight wanes, the leaves hold tight,
Planning adventures long into the night.
A leafy council convenes on the edge,
Making pacts while sitting on the ledge.

With shadows creeping, they start to play,
Joking about the end of a sunny day.
They wiggle and squirm, taking their bow,
Under the glow, oh, how they wow!

Each petal a comedian, sharing their tales,
With laughter that echoes like train whistles wails.
Draped in twilight, their spirits rise,
Nature's embrace under starry skies.

So here's to the fun, from dusk till dawn,
Where silence is rare, and laughter goes on.
With every rustle, a punchline waits,
In the glow of the night, humor elates.

Tapestry of Flora

A patchwork of green hangs high on the wall,
Like nature's quilt, ready for a fall.
In the loom of the room, they twist and they weave,
Creating a scene that you won't believe.

Each leaf a character, zany and wild,
Trying to woo the sun, just like a child.
They giggle and wiggle in the fresh spring air,
A tapestry bright, without a care.

The petals gossip and share their best lines,
As laughter erupts over greens and their vines.
In this botanical dance, skits come alive,
Nature's comedy club, where all can thrive.

So let's celebrate plants, in all their delight,
Their whimsical ways, from morning till night.
For the tapestry shifts, with laughter and glee,
In the crafting of life, they're as funny as can be.

The Ceiling of Leaves

Leaves do a dance with the light,
Swinging like chandeliers, quite a sight.
Silly squirrels scamper with glee,
Thinking they own this leafy spree.

They wiggle, they jiggle, oh what a show,
Draped like curtains, they'll steal the glow.
Imagine the stories they whisper and sway,
While critters below dream their day away.

A rogue branch drops, a hearty jest,
Landing on heads, a nature's quest.
Chuckles erupt from all around,
As laughter bounces from ceiling to ground.

So next time you glance at what hangs above,
Remember the antics from nature with love.
Ceilings can't hold all the humor and glee,
As leaves flutter down, playful and free.

Veils of Verdancy

Veils of greenplay twist and twirl,
Like hula hoops whirling in a whirled.
A comical scene, a leafy parade,
Nature's own show, with no need for aid.

Laughter erupts from a nearby bench,
As vines tickle souls with a gentle wrench.
They tangle and twist, an acrobatic flair,
Inviting the world to stop and stare.

The sun peeks through, a spotlight bright,
On the leafy performers in fanciful flight.
With each little leaf doing its best,
Who knew greenery could cause such a jest?

So let's raise a toast to those floating leaves,
Who remind us to giggle and never reprieves.
For life's too short to dwell in the dense,
Let's dance with nature, it's all so immense!

Overhead Embrace

An overhead embrace that looks quite odd,
Like a green octopus giving a nod.
It reaches and stretches, enthusiastic flair,
Holding the ceiling with garden affair.

"Watch your head!" shouts a friend with a grin,
As a branch swings low, inviting a spin.
Nature's acrobat, playing the part,
Bringing a chuckle straight from the heart.

Floral surprises, blooms on the prowl,
Like cheeky kittens, they wiggle and howl.
A dance with the shadows, bright and absurd,
In this grand spectacle, laughter's inferred.

So look up, dear friends, at the roof above,
Where playful greens mingle, a gift of love.
Under this canopy, life's never quite bland,
With foliage prancing, it's all perfectly planned!

Life's Intricate Tapestry

A tapestry spins from woven greens,
Each tendril a tale, full of scenes.
Chasing the rays like playful sprites,
With every twist bringing delight sights.

A patchwork of giggles, a canvas of cheer,
Nature's own jesters that dance without fear.
Who knew a foliage could host a fair,
Where the punchline's wrapped in the morning air?

Like a knitted odd sock that's lost all its mates,
Leaves weave together to form funny fates.
With whispers of jokes held tight in those fronds,
The humor grows wildly, it genuinely bonds.

So join in the laughter, let's share in this art,
As life's vines and branches playfully part.
Remember the moments when joy's on display,
In this quirky tapestry, come out and play!

The Ceiling's Lush Secrets

In corners, they plot and twine,
Like roommates who don't pay a dime.
They stretch their limbs in leafy cheer,
While claiming space we hold dear.

A jungle gained without a fight,
They giggle in the fading light.
With tendrils that dance in the breeze,
They raise a toast to all with ease.

From dust bunnies they make their bed,
And whisper jokes that tickle the head.
Who knew plants had a sense of fun?
Their pranks are not yet done!

So let them grow in wild delight,
As shadows skip and giggles ignite.
With every inch they weave anew,
We find our ceiling's lively crew.

Flora's Silent Song

In the quiet, whispers arise,
From leafy tips to curious eyes.
They croon a tune of mischief and play,
As they stretch across in their own way.

With every twist a giggle's born,
Surprising us each early morn.
Pretending they're great acrobats,
Swinging like carefree acrobat cats.

The light above their leafy face,
Turns nonchalance into a race.
They tickle the fans with a gentle tease,
While dancing with the softest breeze.

They laugh as they climb and sway,
Inviting all to join the play.
Nature's jesters in a green parade,
Their antics are never to fade.

Celestial Vegetation

These leafy souls above our heads,
In whims and giggles, they spread threads.
Like nature's clowns on a high wire,
With every sway, they conspire.

We look up, and they look down,
With leafy grins, they wear a crown.
Their leafy pranks spread cheer galore,
Who thought the sky would host a store?

In shadows, they play hide and seek,
While sunbeams light their leafy peak.
With every whisper and every sway,
They throw surprises our way.

So let them sing from heights so grand,
In every twist, they're not bland.
A canopy of humor we adore,
Elevated antics, never a bore!

The Enchanted Overhead

Oh what a sight, above our head,
An artful mess where few have tread.
With curls and twists they make their mark,
Creating laughter in the dark.

They hang like clowns on invisible wires,
As bright as the sun, as wild as fires.
With leaves that flounce in cheeky glee,
They tease the air, so playfully free.

In their realm, the ceiling beams,
They drench the room in leafy dreams.
With shenanigans, they cause a stir,
A rooftop party; look at her!

So gaze above with open eyes,
Where laughter and green love lies.
These lively spirits, ever so bold,
Are the stories that need to be told.

Wild Growth Above

There's a jungle up high, it seems,
My living room's turned into dreams.
A plant has taken my hat away,
I wear a fern now, I must say.

The light cords dance in a leafy waltz,
My cat stares up, it's his new vault.
Each morning brings a leafy surprise,
Who knew my home was a green disguise?

The curtains swear they're not in league,
Yet here they are, causing fatigue.
Can't find the remote, it's gone astray,
Maybe it's hiding in the bouquet.

As I sip tea under the green show,
I wonder how far this chaos will grow.
My ceiling's now a garden diorama,
I chuckle softly, it's pure melodrama.

Nature's Embrace Above

Look up! What's that? A leafy parade,
My ceiling's become a nature escapade.
Every morning, I'm greeted by vines,
Plotting to take over my fancy designs.

Sticky notes cling to their leafy grip,
I lose my balance, might take a trip.
Plants whisper secrets, what do they know?
Plotting world domination, or just for show?

I trip on a palm while searching for snacks,
My living room looks like a scene from the tracks.
Who needs a store when my home's a zoo?
I'll soon charge visitors just for the view!

In this botanical chaos, I'm supreme,
Ruler of weeds? Oh, what a dream.
Next week I'll try to teach them some grace,
But for now, there's a fern in my face!

Skyward Tangles

I gazed up high, what a curious sight,
There's a green mess grabbing all the light.
It seems that the plants conspired in glee,
To turn my abode into a green spree.

My ceiling fan now wears a leafy crown,
Who knew my top was the town's new gown?
My guests just laugh when they come to play,
No more blue sky, just a jungle ballet.

Each morning brings the struggle anew,
To find the coffee, or a shoe or two.
A dance of leaves, a shimmering game,
I'm convinced my plants are all to blame.

So here I sit, in my plant-filled bliss,
While ferns conspire for their next big wish.
One day I'll tame this green madness above,
But for now, it's chaos, and I'm filled with love!

Draped in Green

Above my head, a wild carpet thrives,
Where did the ceiling go? It dives and jives.
The curtains are wresting with a peasoup vine,
And it seems like the ivy is plotting a sign.

My chandelier's lost in a leafy embrace,
Each evening I wonder if I should brace.
Will my dinner guests get trapped in the green?
Or will they consider it part of the scene?

I comb through the greenery, looking for clues,
What's hiding up there, what old dusty shoes?
A taco eludes me, it sways with disdain,
Guess I'll have to order another from the train!

So here in my jungle, I gather the fun,
Underneath the chaos, I can't help but run.
If you're craving laughter, come take a peek,
At my nature's circus, it's quite the freak!

Crooked Pathways Above

A spider spun a web so bright,
It danced and twirled in morning light.
The cat thought it was quite a game,
To pounce and prance without much fame.

Each twist and turn, a tangled mess,
A playground where the critters press.
With laughter echoing through the air,
They leap and dive without a care.

The sunbeams tickle leaves so green,
A canopy where dreams convene.
Among the chaos, giggles swell,
As everyone knows, this madcap spell.

When squirrels swing with reckless glee,
You'd think they danced with cups of tea.
With every swing, a hearty cheer,
Join the fun—I'll bring the beer!

The Echoing Green

In the garden, where laughter reigns,
The tomatoes wear their tiny chains.
Whispers float like clouds on high,
As veggies scheme to touch the sky.

A raccoon dons a leafy hat,
While chasing shadows, oh what's that?
A rogue potato rolls with glee,
Declaring war on the carrot spree!

The daisies are all in on it too,
With shaky leaves, they laugh anew.
Each bloom a character in this play,
They sway and giggle throughout the day.

Though bees buzz loud in endless flight,
Their hum becomes a comic light.
In this green stage, a wild display,
Nature's jesters come out to play.

Rustling Secrets Above

The branches creak in joyous cheer,
As secrets rustle, drawing near.
A squirrel's tale about last night's feast,
In laughter's grip, we're all released.

The leaves gossip, sharing their finds,
About the humans and their kinds.
"Did you see their clumsy dance?"
The trees chuckle; they take a chance.

A breeze swoops in with jokes to tell,
Setting the scene, all is well.
The songs of birds rise with the sun,
While squirrels scatter, spry and fun.

From the rooftop, a neighbor yells,
While the garden grows its leafy swells.
Up here, we see the world below,
In flipping leaves, a funny show.

Unfurling the Sky

So here we stand, the bold and bright,
With tendrils reaching for height.
As clouds drift by with fluffy flair,
We pose like models, without a care.

The birds above start taking bets,
On which will win in playful sets.
A race of roots with silly aim,
Competing in this leafy game.

The sun winks down, a cheeky grin,
As petals flutter, drawing in.
"Onward!" they shout, as fun unfolds,
To tickle blooms with tales retold.

With every twist, there's joy and jest,
As nature thrives, at its very best.
In tangled laughter, life's sweet song,
With wonders shared, we all belong.

Whispers of Green Tendrils

In the corner, sneaky leaves,
Waving like they've got their keys.
They tickle the cat, cause a scene,
"Hey, don't munch on my small green beans!"

Twisting around the old lamp base,
Trying hard to win the race.
"Dude, we're not in a jungle vibe,"
Said the rug, while it tried to bribe.

The curtains sway, a leafy dance,
Catch them, they might take a chance.
"Is it a plant or some lost yarn?"
Laughter blooms—a nature barn.

Rolling in static like a clown,
These leafy pranks can't bring you down.
"Hey! Not on the TV remote!"
Broke the silence with a little joke!

Shadows Drape the Air

Shadows bouncing off the wall,
As plants plot a funny sprawl.
"Let's hide the snacks, that'd be fun!"
A vine grinned, "Oh, get it done!"

They twirl around and take a leap,
Creeping stealthily, not a peep.
"Who knew they were such little spies?"
Snickered a pot with bulbous eyes.

A leaf slipped down with a carefree fling,
Lands in a bowl, what a silly thing!
"Don't blame me, it was the breeze!"
Chaos giggles among the leaves.

Webs of shadows, chatty and bold,
In their mischief, laughter unfolds.
Plant life living their best charade,
Who knew a garden could be so played?

Elysian Canopy

Underneath this leafy dome,
The laughter ripples like a foam.
"Just look at them—got style and flair!"
Said the table, with utmost care.

"Watch that one, creeping up high!"
It challenges every passerby.
"Let go of my drink," cried out the stool,
A plant's antics look like a fool!

When they grab the ceiling tight,
And sway all day, what a sight!
"Who ordered this leafy circus show?"
Chided a chair with a wobbly flow.

As the sun beams, they start to prance,
With twirls and twigs, they'll take their chance.
"Join our cabaret, beneath the hue!"
Chuckled a leaf, "We'll make it too!"

Interwoven Dreams

In this tangled web of cheer,
Leaves enact their own chandelier.
"Wow, look at all the twists and bends,"
Said the floor, "These are my new friends!"

Hitching rides on the lampshade,
Every plant has now parlayed.
"A bit too cozy, I might say,"
Grumbled the lightbulb, in dismay.

With whispers soft, they share a jest,
"Shush!" said the wall, "Give it a rest!"
But the leaves just laughed and swayed,
In their crazy vine parade.

As night falls, there's a leafy glow,
They scheme and plan, "Where next to go?"
"Who's up for a climb on the door?"
A potted plant roared, "Let's explore!"

Entwined in the Ether

In the corner hangs a mop,
With dreams of being a vine.
It sways and tries to bop,
Under disco lights that shine.

The ceiling fans join in,
Spinning tales of the grand.
A dance-off with a grin,
As dust bunnies take a stand.

A lonely shoe lost track,
Hoping to find a pair.
It twirls to get back,
But ends up in the air!

A clock with no clear time,
Tick-tocks to the beat.
Its rhythm, oh so prime,
Makes every moment sweet.

Celestial Canopy

A disco ball's bright gleam,
Hangs low like a comet.
With reflections in a dream,
It laughs—oh, what a sonnet!

The walls are in a craze,
As laughter starts to sprout.
Each creak ignites a blaze,
Of giggles all about.

The curtains wave hello,
In a waltz with the breeze.
They tango, twirl, and flow,
Bring a laugh with such ease.

A rubber plant with flair,
Tells jokes from times long gone.
The ceiling can't compare,
To this green, talkative spawn.

Nature's Reach

The window thinks it's cool,
With the sunbeams on its face.
It acts like a wise fool,
Playing card games in space.

An old broom takes a spin,
Sings songs from yesterday.
It grins with a cheeky grin,
'Come join my sweeping ballet!'

Mismatched socks start to sway,
In a party of their own.
Hoping for a fun day,
To shake off all their moans.

The lamp joins the delight,
Flickering 'like' and 'love.'
It dances all night bright,
Under stars from above.

Lush Twists of Fate

A pickle jar quite bold,
Hopes someday to be found.
With stories to be told,
It sits safely, quite sound.

A paperclip is the star,
Bending claims to some fame.
It snares a drink from afar,
In this wild, funny game.

A curtain tries to snooze,
But the breeze gives a shove.
It twists and does the blues,
In a dance fit for love.

Beneath all this ruckus,
The ceiling knows it well.
For laughter's the focus,
In this comical spell.

Threads of Eden

In the corner, they twist and twine,
A leafy party, oh so divine.
They sneak past my coffee cup,
Calling me out for a little sup.

When I stretch for a snack, oh what a sight,
Pasta's not from me, but the vine took flight.
They wave and dance in the morning glow,
Sipping sunlight, putting on a show.

Each tendril whispers secrets sweet,
Creeping closer, oh what a feat!
Should I twist them or set them free?
Or perhaps they want my next cup of tea?

With each loop, my ceiling's now framed,
A green spaghetti, who knows it's named?
In this Eden, I can't help but cheer,
Plant your feet, it's a wild frontier!

Overhead Entanglements

In the hallway, what a mess!
The green brigade is such a guess.
They hang like chandeliers, so delight,
Daring me to take a bite!

Dark green curls above my head,
Do I want them on toast, or in bed?
They giggle down from the light,
Calling me to join their flight.

Suspended high, they plot and scheme,
Just a plot twist in my dream.
Sometimes they tickle and make me sneeze,
I laugh while dodging as they tease.

With a flair for the dramatic, they swing,
Creating chaos, oh what a thing!
In this jungle, I might just fall,
But what a story, I'll tell them all!

In the Heart of Greenery

Look up! What do you see?
A forest canopy, wild and free.
Each petal and leaf with jesters' glee,
Spinning tales of their jubilee.

They leap and twirl, a comical crew,
Like circus acrobats, what a view!
While I'm here just trying to relax,
They laugh at my awkward snacks.

A green can-can in the afternoon,
Waltzing vines, a funny tune.
Who knew my ceiling could become a stage?
Filled with whimsy, full of rage!

Dancing through life, so spry and bold,
Turning mundane to tales of old.
In giggles and sighs, they flourish free,
And I can't help but join in glee!

A Dance in the Upper Realm

Up above, a vibrant spree,
With faux pas vines swaying with glee.
They stomp and prance, daring a leap,
Whispering secrets, none too deep.

As I munch, they cast a spell,
Creating mischief, oh what the hell!
With rolls and twirls, they steal the scene,
Drawing laughter from green cuisine.

I shout, "Not my sandwich, you sly vine!"
But they're just here for the good old time.
Around my snack, they twist and scheme,
Planning a takeover, or so it seems.

In the end, who can complain?
For laughter and laughter, they reign!
These larks and ferns in their grand ball,
Who knew the ceiling could bounce so tall?

The Weight of Existence in Green

In the corner, plants have grown,
Hanging leaves that moan and groan.
They tickle me as I walk by,
I swear they're plotting, oh my my!

Snaking down from ledges high,
Whispers of vines make me sigh.
They seem to giggle, play their part,
A leafy circus, growing art.

The rubber plant wears a frown,
While spider plants dance up and down.
Who knew greens had such a flair?
A leafy comedy laid bare!

So here I sit beneath this sway,
With plants that watch me everyday.
They laugh at life, oh what a scene,
In this madness, I'm their queen.

Ceiling of Nature's Embrace

Up above, a tangled mess,
Nature's fingers in a dress.
They reach out, whisper, tease my hair,
I duck and dodge but don't despair.

A fern's ambition is quite grand,
To conquer this uncharted land.
Each twist and turn, a daring feat,
I think they're plotting to take a seat.

And when the sunlight starts to gleam,
They look alive, in my wild dream.
Shadows dance in pure delight,
These flora jesters, oh what a sight!

I giggle at their leafy prance,
As they sway in a leafy dance.
Who knew my ceiling could emit,
Such laughter in a verdant wit?

Tendrils of Time

Time marches on, but look above,
A twisty party, oh how they shove!
Each tendril seeks a sunny spot,
They care not for the thoughts I've got.

Climbing high, they share some jokes,
With every leaf, they pull my hoax.
A tangled web of green delight,
Making plans far out of sight.

I poke a branch and it sways back,
A leafy friend that's on the attack.
Do they conspire with the clock?
I ponder while I sip my frock.

A life of green, a twisty tale,
Where laughter stretches like a trail.
These charming greens, they steal the show,
In tangled fun, they only grow!

Whispered Shadows Above

Above my head, a mystery grows,
With whispered tales nobody knows.
The leaves conspire in secret code,
    Plotting mischief on my abode.

A shadow darts, I feel the brush,
As plants above begin to hush.
They tease the light, a game they play,
    While I look on in stunned dismay.

Wispy lines that tickle the air,
A leafy prank, a rustic flair.
I chuckle at this green charade,
In nature's grip, I've been displayed.

So here I sit, bemused and bright,
With nature's jests on this fine night.
These verdant sprites keep me alive,
    In shadows above, I truly thrive!

Forgotten Greenery

In the corner, a plant did rise,
With leaves like fingers, waving hi.
Dusty and lost, it sings so sweet,
To the rhythm of cats, beneath its feet.

A hunter in the wild, it seems to jest,
Sprouting from coffee cups, it's quite the guest.
Each time I pass, it whispers a tune,
A serenade to the lazy noon.

Twisting in chaos, a room's delight,
It questions my sanity, day and night.
"Water me, please!" it seems to pout,
But I can't tell if it's in or out.

Here's to the green that doesn't care,
A leafy wonder without a prayer.
In every crevice, it finds a seat,
A forgotten friend, so bittersweet.

Ties to the Sky

There's something wild up in the air,
Green tentacles dance without a care.
Like a toddler's art, it goes awry,
A jumbled mess that reaches high.

It curls around the light so strong,
The bulbs just hum a silly song.
If I poke it gently, will it bite?
Or just giggle in the shimmering light?

Neighbors pass, their jaws drop low,
"A jungle in there?" they quizzically crow.
I shrug and grin, "It's my new pet!"
A leafy creature, the best one yet.

With every twist, it spreads its cheer,
Attracting the birds, oh dear, oh dear!
"Keep it down, folks!" I try to shout,
But it's too busy giving hugs out.

The Dappled Light Above

Oh look at that! A leafy crown,
Swaying gently, up and down.
It tickles my thoughts, a green ballet,
A show for the sun throughout the day.

Every shadow tells a joke or two,
A cast of characters - who knew?
Beams of sunlight peek and play,
"Join the fun!" I hear them say.

Cacti giggle, ferns roll their eyes,
While dangling tendrils act so sly.
A whimsical world above my head,
Where laughter plants and pets are fed.

So let the branches twist and twirl,
In this green chaos, my thoughts unfurl.
With every loop, a wink, a twist,
A garden of humor too good to miss.

Interwoven Dreams

In a tangle of green, I spot a whim,
Ribbons of joy with a quirky grin.
Under the arch of this leafy spree,
A carnival of colors just for me.

The whimsy curls, a playful tease,
Hiding a world of giggles and ease.
"Don't you dare trim!" I sternly scold,
"Each loop's a story waiting to be told."

They frolic and twist in a cheerful mess,
Creating a ceiling that's anyone's guess.
Amidst the laughter, I sip my tea,
In this jungle hideout, wild and free.

Though tangled and wild, it brings such glee,
For dreams are born where the green will spree.
Together we laugh, in our leafy dome,
In this cozy chaos, I feel at home.

Green Enchantment

In my room, a plant took flight,
Over the lamp, it danced at night.
I swear it giggled, swung with glee,
Sipping the sun like a cup of tea.

Leaves made hats, how they would twirl,
It whispered secrets, gave a whirl.
Bobby pinned on that leafy crown,
Now I'm the queen of this green town!

Shadows and Sunbeams

Oh look, a shadow, it winks at me,
As sunbeams play hide-and-seek with glee.
The curtain sways, it flirts with light,
What a show, it's quite the sight!

My cat leaps high, he's in the game,
Chasing sunspots, never feels the shame.
They scatter fast, tease with delight,
He pounces, then they vanish from sight.

Rising Dreams

In the corner, a dream took root,
It climbed and climbed, oh what a hoot!
Twisted and turned, it reached the beams,
Spinning tales from growing dreams.

Each leaf a wish, each stem a hope,
Scaling heights, it learned to cope.
Sometimes it trips, sometimes it slips,
Yet laughs aloud, as nature flips.

Life's Looming Tapestry

Threads of laughter weave through time,
As life's odd patterns start to chime.
One knot's a friend, another's a foe,
Unraveled tales with a funny glow.

Around the bends, surprises hide,
With each new twist, we take the ride.
Loop-de-loops and twirly swirls,
Life's a dance with joyful twirls!

Green Canopy Dreams

In my living room a jungle grows,
With leafy friends striking silly poses.
They shimmy and shake with such carefree flair,
But my cat thinks it's time for a leafy affair.

Pothos on shelves, they're having a ball,
Swinging like monkeys, just waiting to fall.
I swear they giggle when I'm not around,
Plotting a takeover of this funny ground.

Sunlight dances on foliage bright,
A circus of growth, what a wild sight!
Their roots are tangled in a lively spree,
Creating a circus up there just for me.

Oh, the tales they weave from dusk until dawn,
These plants make me wonder if I'm still lawn.
A green canopy dreaming of heights to unroll,
Whispering secrets that tickle my soul.

Climbing to the Light

Up the wall they go, these plants that tease,
Reaching for sunshine with delicate ease.
They've got ambitions, oh what a sight,
Daring the ceiling to lend them some light!

One little tendril just won't stay still,
Trying to dance while I'm sipping my frill.
What's that? A party? Oh, they want to invite,
Every insect and critter to join in the flight!

The more they grow, the more they relay,
Stories of mischief from day to day.
"Let's mess with the curtains," they giggle and plot,
As I scramble to catch them—oh, they're always a lot!

Climbing to funny heights with no thought of fear,
I'm joined by my plants, a raucous cheer!
With every new leaf, the laughter ignites,
A green parade marching to new funny heights!

Nature's Latticework

The room is a patchwork of green and delight,
Leaves intertwining in a comical fight.
They wiggle and jive as they stretch for the sky,
Wearing an aura of mischief nearby.

Every planter's home has its own little scheme,
As they plot their ascent with a whimsical gleam.
Beneath the green cover, there's laughter galore,
Plants playing tag from the ceiling to floor!

If foliage could talk, oh the tales they would spin,
Of adventures they've had—where to even begin?
From awkward encounters with my short little chair,
To the wild escapades of climbing the air!

Nature's artwork hangs mid-laughter-filled days,
Turning my space into a leafy ballet.
With joy in the air and greens in the mix,
Life's just a comedy, a green little fix!

Cascading Greenery

From the shelves they cascade, a green waterfall,
Each leaf a performer ready to sprawl.
They twist and twirl in this wild dance of fate,
Pestering my cat and stealing his plate!

Oh, how they giggle as they scatter around,
Making my home their home, a leafy playground.
From creeping on counters to climbing my shoes,
These plants have a flair for the antics they choose!

The light filters through like a whimsical song,
While they plot and plan—how could this go wrong?
With each little sprout comes a riot of cheer,
As they orchestrate chaos, we share out a beer!

Cascading greenery, what a charming array,
Crafting a circus in their leafy ballet.
They frolic and play all under my roof,
In a world built of laughter—oh, what a goof!

Overarching Tales

In a room where shadows play,
A plant decided it would sway.
It stretched its arms with clumsy grace,
And left the lights in a twisted lace.

The lamp screamed out, 'Oh, let me go!'
As leaves did tangle toe to toe.
My coffee pot now sings a tune,
While hoping it won't bloom too soon.

The chair's in shock, the rug's in fright,
As plants conspire in the night.
They laugh and wriggle, swell with glee,
Who knew decor could dance so free?

So gather 'round, enjoy the show,
These leafy jokers steal the flow.
Their antics leave us all in stitches,
As nature's whim unwittingly glitches.

The Nature's Canopy

A leafy lark took center stage,
With vines that seemed to act their age.
They swung and swayed, a leafy crew,
Hosting a party just for you!

The chandelier was in dismay,
As greens began their wild ballet.
They tickled lampshades, stole the shine,
And danced atop the glass—divine!

"Oh tidy up!" the rug did shout,
"Stop swinging like you're on a route!"
But laughter echoed off the walls,
As leaves cascaded, nature calls.

So raise a glass to leafy friends,
Whose fun and frolic never ends.
They bring a cheer, a cheerful spree,
Under this vibrant canopied glee.

Leaves in The Limelight

Beneath the bulb's fluorescent glow,
Leaves start their step, a quirky show.
With twirls and leaps, they hit their mark,
Broadcasting folly, bright and stark.

One leaf tripped on a nearby cup,
With a dramatic, flailing up.
"Not my fault," it croaked with flair,
"Just testing if the air is fair!"

The curtains rustled, doors did creak,
As leafy performers found their peak.
Who knew a plant could be so spry?
Even the walls began to sigh.

Applaud the daring, green brigade,
In this music hall, they serenade.
With leaves aloft, in joy we steep,
Together in this rhythm, leap!

Tangles of Tranquility

In corners where dust bunnies play,
Tangled greens would not delay.
They snickered soft with leafy breath,
In a twisted game of leafy deft.

"Watch me loop-de-loop!" cried a sprout,
While others cheered, without a doubt.
They climbed and twirled in jester's jest,
A leafy circus, simply the best!

A pot of soil claimed, "This won't do!"
As roots combined in a leafy stew.
Who knew tranquility came with strife,
In nature's mischief, they found life.

So here we sit with laughter brimming,
While leafy larks keep tuning, singing.
These tangled greens, a funny spree,
In harmony, they're wild and free!

Luminous Labyrinths

In the corners, shadows play,
Twisting light in a quirky sway,
A spider's web with flair and grace,
Dancing dust, a lively space.

Green tendrils stretch, they twist and twine,
Draped in laughter, oh so fine,
Like silly hats on pets at noon,
They brighten rooms, make hearts attune.

Whispers echo with every sway,
Each leaf has secrets of the day,
Caught in smiles, tangled in cheer,
These indoor jungles bring us near.

So watch your step, make no mistake,
Each turn could spark a giggle quake,
In glowing paths where shadows tease,
Life's a maze—just enjoy the breeze.

Earthbound Aspirations

At dawn they stretch to greet the sun,
Plant socks in dirt, say life is fun,
They giggle at the birds on high,
Wishing for wings, a joyful sigh.

With every twist, a harmless prank,
Leaves flash mischief, in rows and rank,
They dream of trips through skies so blue,
While sipping rain like morning dew.

Hitching rides on old porch beams,
They're daring us to join their dreams,
Laughter swells like popcorn pops,
As tiny tendrils take their hops.

So let's unwind and join their game,
In the wild dance, there's no shame,
For on this earth, we too can reach,
Life's a lesson, let joy teach.

Clinging to Possibility

They reach for heights, those daring greens,
With wild ambitions that tease our schemes,
Swaying softly like a humorous dance,
Reminding us all to take a chance.

With each new twist and playful curl,
They celebrate life, spin and twirl,
Throwing caution to the playful breeze,
Chasing dreams with such silly ease.

Wrapped around books and old guitars,
They strum the air, send dreams to Mars,
A comedy show beneath the lights,
Their laughter floats to dizzy heights.

So here's to growth and silly ways,
To clinging dreams on sunny days,
Let's join the fun, let's not conform,
For life's a stage—let's all perform!

Above it All

Look up and see the leafy jest,
Nature's stand-up at its best,
Each green leaf shares a witty tale,
Floating high on a breezy sail.

They tease the ceiling, stretch and twist,
Lap up sunshine, none can resist,
Making shadows like wild beasts,
A leafy circus, laugh-fests, feasts.

With carefree hearts, they whirl and swerve,
A leafy crew with nerve and verve,
Sharpened wit like a cactus thorn,
In this leafy world, we're all reborn.

So, take a seat and join the show,
As vines plot fun where giggles flow,
In this high world, where smiles enhance,
Let's sway with greens in a leafy dance.

The Canopy of Breath

In the living room, plants get bold,
They twist and twirl, stories unfold.
A fern took a selfie, reclining with flair,
While my cat gives them all quite a stare.

My eyes go wide as the ivy climbs high,
It seems to be reaching for the pie.
But ten inches up, it finds a mistake,
As the lamp cords now tremble and shake.

Every time I walk by, I can't help but tease,
These leafy acrobats, pushing the breeze.
With jokes and giggles, they sway in delight,
Making my mundane feel silly and bright.

Shall I offer them drinks, maybe tea with lime?
Or set up a stage for their leafy prime time?
In this jungle of green, laughter arrives,
As the room sways and giggles, the spirit thrives!

Silent Stories Above

Up on the ceiling, a riot of green,
Foliage looms like a secretive scene.
A rogue tendril whispers a tale so sly,
While an old spider winks with a bright, tiny eye.

Little leaves plot a plan to escape,
Conspiring secretly, none can reshape.
They map out the room like a bustling town,
As I think, 'Should I give them a crown?'

Twisting and curling, they giggle and play,
In a comical dance, they steal the day.
As if to say, life's fun when we're bold,
With silly adventures just waiting to unfold.

Up high, they giggle, a sight to behold,
Feeling like mischief-makers, not just plants of old.
With every new leaf, and every new twist,
I'm left in stitches, I can't help but assist!

Splintered Light Through Leaves

Sunlight dances, a lively show,
As shadows stretch, we laugh, oh so slow.
Flickering beams are playing tag,
While the ferns giggle, 'Oh, don't lag!'

In a corner, the pothos declares,
'We're starting a trend with our green flares!'
They twirl with delight, beneath the sun's glow,
While I'm laughing at how fast they grow.

Twists like ribbons in a wild parade,
They're not just plants; they're a leafy charade.
With whispers of humor, they spread out wide,
Sipping on light, with joy as their guide.

Each light beam's mischief, a radiant tease,
Comedic shadows that dance with ease.
In this lively realm of color and cheer,
Funny green tales bring us all near!

The Embrace of Nature

Cuddly leaves take over my space,
Wrapping around, a cheeky embrace.
They hug the furniture; oh, what a sight,
While I ponder if they're friendly or fright.

A monstera grins with its big, toothy smile,
Making my coffee break just worth the while.
With each sip I take, it nods and winks,
'Who knew houseplants could stir up such kinks?'

Chasing the sunlight, they jostle about,
With playfulness splendid, there's never a doubt.
They chatter and giggle, plotting their spree,
While I just observe, sipping tea with glee.

So let's raise a toast to this green, wild crew,
In this whimsical space where might blooms anew.
With laughter and joy, let the fun take flight,
In the embrace of nature, everything feels right!

Clusters of Hopeful Growth

Little tendrils climb with glee,
Hoping for a view, you see.
They peek and stretch, such playful sights,
Tickling rafters with their flights.

A daring leap to grasp a beam,
In leafy dreams, they plot and scheme.
What if they reach a bright new place?
They giggle softly, quicken pace.

Such ambitions in their green embrace,
Who knew the ceiling's such a race?
With every twist and every turn,
These cheeky sprouts seek joy to learn.

When shadows play and daylight's sly,
Their little whispers flit and fly.
Sometimes they tangle, what a mess!
But laughter blooms, and all's no less.

Serenity in Suspended Blooms

Fluffy puffs hang out to chat,
Beneath the light, they wiggle fat.
An unexpected twist of fate,
Who knew the ceiling could be great?

Gentle sway in a breezy dance,
As with every sprout, they prance.
They share tall tales of their ascent,
Chasing sunlight, heaven-sent.

A snicker here, a chuckle there,
Who knew blooms had such flair?
They plot to drop a flower or two,
Just for the sake of good ol' fun, too!

Between the beams, they find delight,
In cozy nooks hidden from sight.
With all this joy above our heads,
We tip our hats to these green threads!

Nature's Quiet Intrigue

Green spies linger in the mist,
With secrets shared, they co-exist.
Tickling each other's leafy tails,
As whispers float on gentle gales.

They lean and stretch, they twist and curl,
In a botanical, leafy swirl.
Who knew such charm could thrive up high?
They raise their cups, give shots to the sky.

We ponder what they see each day,
As humans wander, laugh and play.
Just what mischief might they devise?
A sneaky drop, a most clever surprise!

With every tendril, a hidden jest,
Pulling pranks at their leafy best.
Nature's humor in each growing thread,
We shake our heads at what's overhead.

The Ceiling of Possibility

A world above, full of dreams,
With plans that burst at every seam.
They plot their course with boundless cheer,
Stretching limits, year after year.

"Why not?" they ask, with hopeful grins,
As sunlight filters and laughter spins.
Such ambitions swirl with comic flare,
Trying to reach where few would dare.

With curious minds and cheeky schemes,
They play hide and seek in leafy dreams.
What if we grew a leafy crown?
The rafter's throne, not just a frown!

Colorful dreams, swirling up high,
Each sprout a wish, they love to try.
In this haven where fun is king,
They shout in joy for the joy they bring!

www.ingramcontent.com/pod-product-compliance
Lightning Source LLC
Chambersburg PA
CBHW072135070526
44585CB00016B/1688